Back on Track:
The Global Rail Revival

MARCIA D. LOWE

Carole Douglis, *Editor*

WORLDWATCH PAPER 118
April 1994

THE WORLDWATCH INSTITUTE is an independent, nonprofit environmental research organization based in Washington, D.C. Its mission is to foster a sustainable society—in which human needs are met in ways that do not threaten the health of the natural environment or future generations. To this end, the Institute conducts interdisciplinary research on emerging global issues, the results of which are published and disseminated to decisionmakers and the media.

FINANCIAL SUPPORT is provided by the Geraldine R. Dodge Foundation, W. Alton Jones Foundation, John D. and Catherine T. MacArthur Foundation, Andrew W. Mellon Foundation, Edward John Noble Foundation, Pew Charitable Trusts, Lynn R. and Karl E. Prickett Fund, Rockefeller Brothers Fund, Turner Foundation, Frank Weeden Foundation, and Wallace Genetic Foundation.

PUBLICATIONS of the Institute include the annual *State of the World*, which is now published in 27 languages; *Vital Signs*, an annual compendium of the global trends—environmental, economic, and social—that are shaping our future; the *Environmental Alert* book series; and *World Watch* magazine, as well as the *Worldwatch Papers*. For more information on Worldwatch publications, write: Worldwatch Institute, 1776 Massachusetts Ave., N.W., Washington, DC 20036; or FAX (202) 296-7635.

THE WORLDWATCH PAPERS provide in-depth, quantitative and qualitative analysis of the major issues affecting prospects for a sustainable society. The Papers are authored by members of the Worldwatch Institute research staff and reviewed by experts in the field. Published in five languages, they have been used as a concise and authoritative reference by governments, nongovernmental organizations and educational institutions worldwide. For a partial list of available Papers, see page 55.

DATA from all graphs and tables contained in this book, as well as from those in all other Worldwatch publications of the past year, are available on diskette for use with IBM-compatible computers. This includes data from the *State of the World* series of books, *Vital Signs* series of books, Worldwatch Papers, *World Watch* magazine, and the *Environmental Alert* series of books. The data are formatted for use with spreadsheet software compatible with Lotus 1-2-3, including Quattro Pro, Excel, SuperCalc, and many others. Both 3 1/2" and 5 1/4" diskettes are supplied. To order, send check or money order for $89, or credit card number and expiration date (Visa and MasterCard only), to Worldwatch Institute, 1776 Massachusetts Ave., NW, Washington, DC 20036. Tel: 202-452-1999; Fax: 202-296-7365; E-mail: Worldwatch@igc.apc.org.

Printed on 100-percent non-chlorine bleached, partially recycled paper.

Table of Contents

Introduction 5

Ten Advantages of Rail 9

A Transport Turnaround 18

Reinventing the Rails 26

Cars or Trains: A Closer Look at Costs 34

Keeping the Revival on Track 42

Notes 46

Tables and Figures

Table 1: *Ten Advantages of Rail Over Highway and Air Transport* 11

Table 2: *Comparison of Rail Networks, Selected Countries* 22

Table 3: *Road versus Rail Travel, Selected Countries* 24

Table 4: *Status of High Speed Rail in Selected Countries* 31

Table 5: *Funding Sources for U.S. Highway Spending, 1992* 36

Table 6: *Estimated External Costs of Passenger Transport in Germany* 37

Sections of this paper may be reproduced in magazines and newspapers with written permission from the Worldwatch Institute. For information, call the Director of Communication, at (202) 452-1999 or FAX (202) 296-7365.

The views expressed are those of the author, and do not necessarily represent those of the Worldwatch Institute and its directors, officers, or staff, or of funding organizations.

ACKNOWLEDGMENTS: I would like to thank Ross Capon and Harriet Parcells for their insightful comments on early drafts. I am also grateful to Lori Baldwin for helping with the research, and to Christopher Flavin for providing project oversight.

MARCIA D. LOWE is a Senior Researcher at the Worldwatch Institute, where she analyzes urban transport and land use issues. She is coauthor of five of the Worldwatch Institute's *State of the World* reports, and author of Worldwatch Paper #98, *Alternatives to the Automobile: Transport for Livable Cities*, and Worldwatch Paper #105, *Shaping Cities: The Environmental and Human Dimensions*. Ms. Lowe holds a master's degree in appropriate technology and energy management from the Department of City and Regional Planning at the University of Pennsylvania.

Introduction

On January 17, 1994, a severe earthquake hit Los Angeles, California, toppling key bridges and crippling the region's highway system. Perhaps even more earth-shaking than the 6.8-magnitude quake, however, was what happened in the aftermath: There in the land of the automobile, thousands of drivers left their cars at home and clambered onto commuter trains. Ridership on one line increased more than 20-fold, compelling officials to expand service and erect five emergency stations in two weeks. One longtime rider on the Metrolink rail system—inaugurated in 1992—marvelled at the unusual crush of passengers: "It looked like they were filming a movie," he said.[1]

But the rail rush did not last. Commuters flocked back to the roads as soon as detours were opened and freeways repaired. Railway officials had projected that train ridership would taper off once the major thoroughfares were restored, but the decline was even sharper than expected. Barely a month after the quake, Metrolink ridership had slipped to some 20,000 passengers a day—double that before the temblor, but far below the post-quake peak—and is almost sure to shrink further as commuters fall back into their old driving habits. The region seems to have missed a golden opportunity to break free of its infamous auto dependence and accompanying fuel waste, smog, and traffic jams.[2]

The recent L.A. experience contains valuable lessons applicable to much of the world today as government after government turns to railway expansion following decades of nearly exclusive focus on highway building. Sweden plans to invest as much in railways as in roads during the coming decade, and Germany plans investment in rail to exceed that in roads through the year 2010. Twelve European countries recently agreed on a $76-billion proposal to link major cities with nearly 30,000 kilometers of high-speed rail lines, and governments are trying to unclog the continent's highways by switching some of the truck freight onto trains. Even in the United States, high-speed train service is under consideration for several long distance routes, and a number of cities are adding or expanding rail systems.[3]

Like the turnaround in post-earthquake Los Angeles, the global rail revival is propelled by a crisis: not a sudden disaster, but a steady worsening of air quality and traffic congestion. The cities and countries now trying to expand the role of rail face a challenge similar to that in Los Angeles: achieving a permanent shift to trains in a transport environment rigged to favor driving.

If planners were to dream up a clean, efficient, and safe transport system for societies the world over, they would be hard pressed to produce a better idea than rail. For every kilometer of travel, an intercity passenger train consumes only one-third as much energy per rider as a commercial airplane, and one-sixth as much as a car carrying only the driver. Commuters who take light rail or the subway to work instead of driving solo slash their contribution to urban smog, cutting nitrogen oxide emissions from each trip by 60 percent and nearly eliminating carbon monoxide and particulate emissions.[4]

Expanding the role of rail would relieve traffic congestion, which not only causes stress and inconvenience but also costs countries billions of dollars a year in lost employee time and delayed delivery of goods. The United States General Accounting Office (GAO) reports that productivity losses from highway congestion cost the nation some $100 billion annually. "Winglock"—the airport equivalent of a traffic jam—represents further costly delays. The International Air Traffic Association estimates that Europe loses $10 billion each year to air traffic tie-ups.[5]

Other major advantages include rail's outstanding safety record. In Japan, between 1964 and 1992, more than 3 billion passenger trips were made on high-speed bullet trains without a fatal accident; the same volume of road travel killed some 2,000 people. In the United States, kilometer for kilometer, the risk of dying in an auto accident is some 18 times greater than the risk of dying in a train accident.[6]

In contrast to highways and airports, which pave over vast expanses of land, railways accommodate passengers and freight in a modest amount of space. Consider, for example, that two railroad tracks can carry as many people in an hour as 16 lanes of highway. And compare Chicago's sprawling O'Hare airport—the world's busiest with 60 million passengers each year—with Paris' Saint-Lazare train station, which handles 150 million passengers in only a fraction of the space. A single large airport takes up more land than some 500 kilometers of the French TGV high-speed rail system.[7]

Rather than the strip malls and sprawling developments that spring up along highways and around airports, urban rail typically encourages compact, higher-value land use. One example is the $70 billion in new apartments, office buildings, and other developments located near the rapid rail lines in otherwise low-density Atlanta, Georgia. Rail stations also help spark redevelopment in urban cores: Victoria Station in London, Brussels' Central Terminal, and Washington, D.C.'s Union Station have all been renovated recently into lively complexes with new offices, restaurants, and shops within and around them.[8]

In Fiscal Year 1994, the U.S. government poured $20.3 billion into highways—nearly 20 times the funding for rail.

Further, trains offer a vital alternative for people who cannot afford a car or airline ticket, or are physically unable to drive or fly. Only an estimated 10 percent of the world's people can afford a car. Flying is the privilege of an even smaller elite, with people in North America and Western Europe—less than 13 percent of the world's population—accounting for nearly three-fourths of global air travel. Even in the highly mobile United States, which nearly has a car for every two people, more than ten million households have no motor vehicle. And an estimated 25 million people nationwide are afraid to fly.[9]

Despite the clear advantages of trains, the global rail revival faces daunting obstacles. Chief among them: Governments in past decades consistently failed to make adequate investments in rail systems. Even West European countries, which have maintained strong train ridership despite fast-growing automobile fleets, spent about three times as much on roads as on rail during the seventies and eighties. Between 1958 and 1989, the U.S. government spent an estimated $213 billion on highways—nearly 10 times as much as on railroads. In recent years, the disparity in U.S. funding between roads and rail has widened even further: In Fiscal Year 1994 the federal government poured $20.3 billion into highways—nearly 20 times the funding for rail.[10]

Not surprisingly, travel patterns reflect these skewed investments. In the United States, for instance, passenger trains account for less than one percent of inter-city travel—a remarkable underuse of capacity, considering that the U.S. rail network is the world's longest. Each year Americans log some 228 kilometers on the road for every kilometer on rail. Canadians, by contrast, travel 76 kilometers by road—and the British 14, the French 8, and the Japanese 2—for every kilometer by train.[11]

Misperceptions of the relative costs of rail and road transport persist. Automobile advocates stress the fact that passenger fares seldom cover the full cost of rail service, so government support of rail remains necessary. Rarely acknowledged, however, is the far greater—though largely hidden—public subsidy of highway transport. In the United States, for example, gasoline taxes, vehicle taxes, and tolls cover less than two-thirds the cost of building, maintaining, and operating highways. The rest— more than $32 billion in 1992—comes from local property taxes, general fund appropriations, and other sources. Combined with the far greater tally for smog, noise, accidents, and other unpaid social costs, the total subsidy to U.S. drivers is estimated at $300-600 billion each year. Recent research in Europe suggests that for every kilometer of travel, the unpaid social cost of cars is twice that of airplanes—and seven times that of trains.[12]

Fortunately, policymakers are coming to realize that rail is a sound investment. But, as post-quake Los Angeles has shown, it takes more than new rail capacity to reform a lopsided transport system. For instance, Los Angeles drivers still enjoy abundant "free" parking and fuel taxes that are among the lowest in the world; these inducements go far to explain why people failed to shake a longstanding preference for driving. And, although new rail lines target major commuting routes, low density development and sprawling urban landscapes create a formidable barrier to attracting train riders. As long as future growth continues in a pattern of sprawl, dependence on cars will only intensify, and a truly comprehensive public transport system will remain elusive.

In Los Angeles and other cities and countries across the globe, ensuring the success of the current rail revival will require bold policy measures. Key steps include:
- raising the price of road transport to more accurately reflect its true costs—from urban smog and global climate change to the pavement damage caused by heavy trucks;
- making it convenient to reach train stations without a car—by improving bus and bicycle access, as well as direct links to airports;
- reforming land use policies to guide future urban growth into less car-dependent patterns.

Ten Advantages of Rail

The most daunting transport problems of the twentieth century can be alleviated by creating diverse transport systems in which rail plays a major role. The term "rail" itself encompasses a wide range of different trains. Passenger travel within cities comes under the heading of urban rail—including heavy rail, or "metro" (running largely in tunnels and on overhead structures), light rail (the modern trolley), and commuter rail (sometimes called regional or suburban service). Most intercity trains travel on national passenger networks. Some of these include high-speed rail lines—in which powerful, aerodynamic trains race between cities along specially designed tracks. Freight trains operate on conventional tracks, many of which are shared by passenger trains.

The various rail options have at least ten major advantages over highway and air transport. Rail's efficient use of energy creates a number of benefits. Other advantages stem from the potential for rail to relieve highway and air traffic congestion. Rail corridors promote optimal use of land and attract development back into urban cores. In addition, rail offers the incalculable social value of far lower accident rates than road transport, and of serving people who are otherwise left out of a system that caters overwhelmingly to drivers. (See Table 1).[13]

Rail's ability to save energy is one of its most important contributions to the environment and to national economies. Trains require less propulsive energy than cars and trucks because of superior aerodynamics and the lower rolling resistance of steel wheels on steel rails. Trains also make fewer stops and speed changes, both of which dissipate energy.[14]

Measured by the energy required to move one passenger one kilometer under U.S. commuting conditions, an intercity train uses some 900 Btu (948 kilojoules)—one-third the energy used by a commercial airplane, and one sixth the energy of an automobile with a sole occupant. Equivalent travel by urban rail uses roughly 1,100 Btu per passenger-kilometer; commuter rail consumes some 1,200.[15]

Moving freight by rail is also more energy-efficient than by road. In the United States, a recent study of intercity freight movement found that, depending on equipment types, terrain, and other factors, trains are 1.4 to 9 times as energy-efficient as trucks. The advantage of hauling more freight by rail is particularly important in developing countries. Older truck models commonly used in the Third World consume 1.5-2.5 times as much energy per ton-kilometer as newer models; poor maintenance, bad road conditions, and traffic congestion further reduce energy efficiency of trucks in poorer countries. [16]

Dependence on oil to fuel road transport greatly strains many nations' balance of payments, making economies vulnerable to swings in the world price of petroleum. As an alternative to private cars, rail can considerably reduce the portion of a country's oil consumption that goes toward transport. In

TABLE 1.

Ten Advantages of Rail Over Highway and Air Transport

Category	Examples
Greater Energy Efficiency	An intercity passenger train is three times as energy-efficient as commercial air and six times as efficent as a car with one occupant.[1]
Less Dependence On Oil	Switching 5 percent of U.S. highway driving to electrified rail would save more than one-sixth the amount of oil imported annually from the Middle East.
Less Air Pollution	For every ton of goods moved one kilometer, freight rail emits one-third the nitrogen oxide and carbon monoxide, and one-tenth the volatile organic compounds and diesel particulates emitted by heavy trucks.
Lower Greenhouse Emissions	For every ton of goods switched from roads to rail in the United Kingdom, the amount of carbon emitted per kilometer would drop by 88 percent.
Less Road & Air Traffic Congestion	Conservative estimates suggest that without Amtrak (the U.S. intercity passenger railroad), air passengers on the New York City/Washington, D.C. route would increase 36 percent.
Fewer Injuries and Deaths	Between 1964 and 1992, more than 3 billion trips were made on Japan's bullet trains without a single fatality; the equivalent volume of road travel over that period killed nearly 2,000 people.
Less Land Paved Over	Two railroad tracks can carry as many people an hour as sixteen lanes of highway. Some 500 kilometers of the French TGV high-speed rail system could fit into the area occupied by a single large airport.
Local Economic Development	In the Washington, D.C. area during the eighties, 40 percent of new building space—worth $3 billion— was built within walking distance of a Metro (subway) stop.
Sustainable Land Use Patterns	Rail corridors help encourage compact, efficient land use. Rail-based cities such as Paris, Stockholm, and Toronto have accommodated new growth while remaining livable and avoiding sprawl and excessive car dependence.
Greater Social Equity	The majority of the world's people can afford neither an automobile nor an airline ticket; rail is a vital option for people who are disabled or too young or old to drive.

[1] Measured by the energy required to move one passenger one kilometer under U.S. commuting conditions.

SOURCE: Worldwatch Institute, based on sources cited in endnote 13.

industrial countries, transport typically accounts for some 30 percent of total oil use. But in China, where bicycles and rail dominate the transport system, only 8 percent of total energy goes to the transport sector. In Eastern Europe, where rail ridership is high and private car ownership low, the figure is 10 percent. Inefficient energy use in these countries' non-transport sectors accounts for some of this difference—industrial, commercial, and residential activities require a disproportionate share of energy—but reliance on energy-efficient rail is a major factor.[17]

Electrifying rail lines—so that trains run on electricity instead of diesel fuel—produces dramatic oil savings. Contrary to popular belief, oil is seldom used to generate electricity. In the former West Germany, for instance, 38 percent of the railways were electrified by 1987; only 2 percent of the electricity was generated by oil. Although many countries have gradually increased the electrified portions of their rail networks, considerable untapped potential remains. Western Europe now has the highest concentration of electrified rail, ranging from 99 percent of intercity rail in Switzerland, to 55 percent in Italy, and 26 percent in the United Kingdom. Thirty-five percent of Japan's intercity network is electrified. The United States lags behind with one percent.[18]

For every passenger carried one kilometer, an intercity train uses one-third the energy of a commercial airplane, and one-sixth the energy of an automobile with a sole occupant.

Regional and local economies are also affected by oil dependence and the composition of the transport sector. In the United States, the states with the least public transportation consume nearly three times as much fuel for transport, per household, as states with extensive rail services. A study by the Los Angeles Regional Transportation Commission shows that 85 cents of every dollar that local residents spend on gasoline leaves the regional economy, much of it leaving the country as well. In contrast, out of every dollar that buys a fare on public transport, an estimated 80 cents goes toward transit workers' wages: Those 80 cents then circulate in the local economy, generating more than $3.80 in goods and services in the region.[19]

Because minimizing energy use minimizes air pollution, an expanded role for rail would help improve air quality. Compared with highway or air travel, diesel-powered rail produces substantially lower amounts of harmful emissions such as carbon monoxide (CO) and volatile organic compounds (VOCs), as well as far less carbon dioxide (CO_2), the main contributor to greenhouse warming. Electrified rail offers even greater reductions, although its full potential to reduce smog and greenhouse emissions is compromised if the electricity is derived from fossil fuels rather than renewables such as wind, solar, or hydropower. For instance in the United Kingdom—where three-fourths of the electricity used in transport comes from coal combustion—electric trains cause higher sulphur dioxide emissions than diesel trains. Carbon emissions attributable to U.K. electric trains, while lower than those from road or air transport, are still roughly the same as those from diesel trains.[20]

Greater reliance on rail would help alleviate traffic congestion on highways and in airports—a problem that results in costly losses of employee time and delays in goods delivery. The Texas Traffic Institute estimates that, in 1988, traffic congestion in U.S. urban areas cost more than $400 per vehicle. In cities in the Northeast, the figure rose to $750 per vehicle. According to the U.S. Office of Technology Assessment (OTA), some federal experts unofficially estimate that congestion costs now equal or exceed federal, state, and local government spending on highways each year. A calculation by the U.S. General Accounting Office found that at the current rate of growth, traffic congestion on roads will triple in 15 years—even if road capacity is increased by 20 percent. And such a massive expansion of capacity is unlikely in any case, given budget constraints and the difficulty of obtaining adequate rights-of-way for major road works.[21]

Shifting freight off crowded roads and onto railways would further relieve congestion. More than one-third of all U.S. freight already travels on tracks; for relatively little extra cost, a far larger share could do so. In 1989, then-Federal Railroad

Administrator Gilbert Carmichael estimated that the U.S. freight rail system was using only a quarter of its capacity. Furthermore, individual railroads can triple their mainline track capacity by improving their train control technologies. They can increase it by up to six times by installing a parallel track along a segment of existing track. Unlike highways, which require median strips, shoulders, and buffers, new tracks can usually be fit into existing rights-of-way.[22]

Rail can also alleviate costly air traffic congestion. Flight delays from crowded air and runway space cost airlines and businesses at least $5 billion annually in the United States. Electrification of the New York-Washington rail corridor enables trains to travel up to 200 kilometers an hour. The speed and relatively low cost help explain why Amtrak, the U.S. national passenger rail service, now carries more passengers than any airline on that route. Using rail to relieve air and highway congestion has a double reward: Since train stations in large cities tend to be downtown, passengers are more likely to use public transport to reach hotels, business meetings, and tourist sites.[23]

Heavier use of rail could render expensive new airports unnecessary, since much of the air space in existing facilities is tied up by short trips easily made by train. Amtrak and the Coalition of Northeast Governors estimate that completing the track improvement and electrification of the Boston-New York corridor will displace 50 flights per day and free up 10 gates at Boston's Logan Airport. Finishing the electrification (which now extends from Washington, D.C. to New Haven, Connecticut) would eliminate the need for Boston's controversial proposed second airport. The rail improvements—including new, high-speed trains—will cost an estimated $1.3 billion, compared to $5-10 billion for a new airport.[24]

Another seldom appreciated benefit is railways' modest appetite for land. Rail requires far less physical space than do highways or airports, so it displaces far fewer homes and jobs. Two railroad tracks can carry the same number of people in an hour as 16 lanes of highway, taking up only 15 meters of right-of-way, compared with roughly 122 meters of roadway width. Highways occupy far more space than typically is recognized. In

1989, the Department of Transport in the United Kingdom produced a plan to construct 2,557 kilometers of highways and
trunk roads. One observer graphically depicted the total land
area needed as equal to a 267-lane highway from London to
Edinburgh—with a parking lot the size of Berkshire at each
end.[25]

Railways hold far greater potential than either airports or
highways to encourage optimal regional land use patterns.
Constructing an airport or highway tends to draw development
out and away from a city. Soon, low-density commercial strips with large
parking lots dominate the landscape.
And, as new homes and businesses
sprawl, it becomes increasingly difficult to move around without a car.
Rail-focused growth, by contrast, lends
itself to more compact and more valuable economic development than the
typical highway offerings of strip malls,
motels, and fast food outlets.

The British Department of Transport puts the cost of each of the country's 5,000-6,000 annual road deaths at $1.3 million.

A rail station placed downtown can
unify a city and attract valuable new development back to older
urban cores. Philadelphia's 30th Street station and Union Station
in Washington, D.C., are examples of newly rehabilitated terminals that have become lively centers filled with restaurants,
shops, and offices. London's renovation of Victoria Station has
produced a thriving commercial complex including office and
retail space built on air rights over the tracks. Rail terminals have
recently been the focus of similar successful redevelopments in
Brussels, Paris, and several other major cities.[26]

Rapidly expanding metropolitan areas can use rail to help
encourage economic vitality and direct anticipated growth.
Montgomery County, Maryland—a county of 740,000 people
near Washington, D.C.—is a case in point. A long-range planning study for the county found that if urban growth continued
in the usual auto- and highway-oriented pattern—even at a
slower pace—the resulting traffic congestion would stifle further economic development. In contrast, focusing most new

urban growth in pedestrian- and bicycle-friendly clusters along an expanded rail and bus system—and revising commuter subsidies to discourage the use of cars—would enable the county to double its current number of jobs and households without exacerbating traffic congestion.[27]

Rail's many benefits include several that, while difficult to quantify, are invaluable to society. One of these is safety. Rail's accident record is much better than that of road transport, despite disproportionate public attention given to the occasional railway accident. In the United States, the risk of death in an auto accident is roughly 18 times that for rail, with 6.67 deaths per 1 billion passenger-kilometers, compared with 0.37 deaths for rail. In the Netherlands and the former West Germany, for every kilometer of road versus rail travel in 1989, road accidents caused 29 times as many deaths and injuries. In France, the per-kilometer road accident toll was 80 times that for rail.[28]

In addition to incalculable health damage and loss of human life, road accidents impose financial burdens. Measures of these costs vary considerably, but may include lost wages; property damage; medical, legal, and administrative charges; and emergency services. The British Department of Transport puts the cost of each of the country's 5,000-6,000 annual road deaths at $1.3 million. Figured as a percentage of gross national product (GNP), estimates of motor vehicle accident costs range from 1.2 percent for several developing countries to 2.4 percent for France, 2.6 for the former West Germany, and 3 percent for Australia. A recent study for the U.S. Federal Highway Administration included estimates of the monetary worth of pain, suffering, and lost quality of life in its tally of the costs of U.S. road accidents in 1988. It arrived at a total of $358 billion, 8 percent of GNP.[29]

Not only passenger but freight trains offer a safety premium. A study by the Organisation for Economic Co-operation and Development (OECD) found heavy trucks more likely than other road vehicles to be in fatal accidents. In contrast, freight train accidents are rare, and, in the United States at least, declining: Between 1980 and 1987, U.S. freight train accident rates fell from 7.3 to 2.9 per million kilometers. The drop is largely thanks to annual investments of $4 billion in renovations and maintenance, and $3 billion in upgrading tracks and equipment.[30]

Rail can also enhance another intangible—the quality of life. For rail passengers, the quiet, rapid ride is a welcome break from chaotic traffic jams. A rail-based transport system also benefits people who do not ride trains: While communities dominated by highways and airports risk becoming mere throughways for people and goods in transit, those traversed by rail are less likely to be disrupted. Interurban rail seldom runs right through residential neighborhoods, but when nearby, it makes a less intrusive neighbor than either highways or airports. And, confined to the track, train traffic does not spill congestion onto nearby arteries and side streets, as road traffic does.

In addition, rail creates less noise than airports or highways. Aircraft noise draws complaints from communities more than 60 kilometers from an airport. In regions crisscrossed by highways and major roads, traffic noise affects large numbers of people. In 13 OECD countries in Europe, the dominant source of noise is road traffic: Nearly 90 percent of residents hear it in their homes. Effects of excessive noise on human health include hearing loss, stress, and interference with rest and sleep. Studies comparing noise generated by rail versus roads show that, when carrying the same load of freight or passengers at the same speed, rail produces on average 25-50 percent less noise than road transport. For freight, the greater goods-hauling capacity of each locomotive makes a dramatic difference in noise level: In the United States, for instance, moving 200 freight containers cross-country would require 3 to 5 locomotives versus 200 trucks.[31]

Finally, rail promotes social equity by providing transportation for people who do not or cannot drive. Few people in low-income developing countries own cars: The number of people per car is 56 in Peru, 113 in Nigeria, and 356 in India. Even in the auto-dependent United States, more than 10 million households have no motor vehicle. And an estimated 10-14 percent of the population in most countries suffers some physical disability that may render them unable to drive. Children and the elderly, many of whom also cannot drive, dominate the demographics in much of the world. All these nondrivers have inferior access to jobs, education, and vital services in car-dominated transport systems. Urban and interurban rail—along with local and regional bus service—therefore provide an indispensable transport option for a significant share of the world's people.[32]

A Transport Turnaround

Since World War II, the role of rail has declined even in countries where it had previously flourished. In the worst cases, rail ceased to be a serious option for transport of passengers or goods as cars and trucks took over in the last few decades. Even in the best instances, governments failed to sustain adequate investment in rail networks, forcing some lines to close and others to reduce the frequency of trains. But today's congested highways, worsening smog, and shortage of land for new roads are reviving official interest in railroads. It will be a long haul for countries that have neglected this important link in their transport systems, but many are beginning to renew their commitment to rail.

Nowhere was the shift away from rail more abrupt than in the United States. In the 1890s, U.S. street railways carried 2 billion passengers a year—more than twice the number served in the rest of the world's cities combined. Then, in the first three decades of this century, more than half of U.S. families acquired automobiles. The massive urban rail network, plagued by declining efficiencies and corruption, was dealt a final blow by a group of corporations in the auto, oil, and rubber tire industries. From the mid-thirties through the forties, several large companies—including General Motors, Standard Oil of California, Phillips Petroleum, Mack Manufacturing (of Mack trucks), and Firestone Tire and Rubber—schemed to acquire and junk the trolley systems of U.S. cities and replace them with buses and cars. A federal court in 1949 convicted the companies of criminal antitrust violations, but it was too late. An important piece of the transport infrastructure had been destroyed—one that cities today are spending billions of dollars to replace.[33]

The combination of popular fascination with cars, federal disinvestment in rail, and outright conspiracy crippled U.S. train travel. With the exception of New York, Chicago, and other large cities that rely extensively on metropolitan rail systems, trains now play a small role in urban transport. Amtrak, the nation's passenger rail system, now accounts for less than one percent of intercity travel. Nevertheless, fast-growing ridership signals that trains are regaining popularity. Travel on Amtrak climbed from 6.8 billion passenger-kilometers in 1982 to just under 10 billion in 1993, an increase of nearly 50 percent.[34]

Freight rail also declined dramatically as the United States shifted goods to trucks. In 1925, railroads carried nearly 80 percent of U.S. intercity freight; by 1992, their share had dropped to an estimated 37 percent. (For comparison's sake, road carries 27 percent; pipeline, 20 percent; water, 16 percent; and air, less than 1 percent.) Yet the United States still moves more of its goods by rail than do its geographically more compact economic competitors: Japan transports 5 percent of its freight by rail; the former West Germany, 22 percent; and France, 24 percent.[35]

In the U.S., travel on Amtrak climbed nearly 50 percent from 1982 to 1993.

Intermodal freight—combining rail and truck transport—is growing quickly in the United States, where long distances favor rail but businesses expect the flexibility of shipping and receiving goods by truck. Special containers that can be hauled by train as well as truck enable shippers to transport goods over long distances economically via rail, then transfer them directly onto trucks for final delivery at widely scattered locations. The railroads' intermodal services have proven so efficient and inexpensive that trucking companies are increasingly relying on rail for the long-haul portion of their shipments. In 1993, the number of intermodal trailers and containers shipped by rail reached nearly 7 million—more than double the number in 1982.[36]

Since the Interstate Highway System was established in 1956, the U.S. government has spent the vast bulk of its ground trans-portation funding on roads. Between 1958 and 1989, federal spending on highways totalled an estimated $213 billion, com-pared with an estimated $23 billion for railroads. In 1990, the federal government poured $13 billion into highways—22 times what it spent on rail. In recent proposals, funding for highways still dwarfs that for train travel, but official interest in both urban and intercity rail is gaining momentum. California has embarked on an ambitious new urban rail program, and high-speed rail is under consideration on routes between several major cities (discussed in the following section, "Reinventing the Rails"). In addition, the current Administration is the first in more than a decade to support increased funding for Amtrak.[37]

West European countries never abandoned their passenger rail systems when the automobile became popular; intercity trains, metros, trolleys, and new light rail systems form an estab-lished part of the landscape and life-styles. The national railways, the largest employer in several countries, represent some of the most comprehensive rail networks in the world.[38]

Freight transport in Western Europe has diminished more sharply than passenger travel. Between 1970 and 1990, rail's share of freight traffic in 14 countries declined from 31 to 17 per-cent, while roads increased their share from 55 to 74 percent—with inland waterways accounting for the remainder. The European Commission estimates that in the new European sin-gle market, between 1990 and 2010 the volume of road freight will have jumped 42 percent. Alarmed about the prospect of "completely unmanageable" highway congestion, the European Community's executive supports shifting as much freight as possible from roads to water and rail.[39]

France, Austria, and Switzerland are particularly interested in diverting freight from roads because of their central position in European trade routes. The Alpine road network, the busiest mountain system in the world, bears 15 percent of Western Europe's goods transport. Reacting to increasing environmen-tal damage from heavy truck traffic, Austria and Switzerland are trying to expand rail capacity on transalpine routes. A 1992 referendum in Switzerland set aside $10.7 billion to build two new Alpine rail tunnels under existing ones. In early 1994, Swiss voters approved another referendum prohibiting the construction of any major new highways and calling for an outright ban on heavy trucks traversing Switzerland en route to other countries. Beginning in 2004, all freight trucks that pass through the country must be rolled onto flatbed railcars.[40]

Railroads in Western Europe seem poised in the nineties to begin recovering from an investment bias toward highways. During the seventies and eighties, 18 European countries spent about 3 times as much on roads as on rail (even though they remained far more committed to rail than the United States, devoting on average 1-1.5 percent of GDP to rail compared with the U.S. range of 0.04-0.07 percent). Sweden intends to invest equal amounts in its railways and roads during this decade, and unified Germany's first transport plan calls for investing more in rail than in roads through the year 2010.[41]

Compared with the United States and Western Europe, Eastern Europe and the former Soviet Union have surrendered little rail capacity to the highway era. Lower consumer buying power, public policies that discouraged private car ownership, and relatively small government investments in highways have kept the region's extensive rail systems largely intact, though often ill-maintained. The former Soviet rail network covers some 150,000 kilometers, second only to the nearly 200,000 kilometers of track in the United States. Before the breakup of the Soviet Union, nearly 45 percent of passenger traffic travelled by rail. And almost 80 percent of freight was carried by rail, a higher share than in any other country. (See Table 2.)

Unfortunately, the former Soviet Republics and countries of

> **In early 1994, Swiss voters approved a referendum prohibiting the construction of any major new highways and calling for an outright ban on heavy trucks traversing Switzerland en route to other countries.**

TABLE 2.

Comparison of Rail Networks, Selected Countries, 1990-1992

Country	Length of Rail Network	Share of Total Freight Traffic	Share of Total Passenger Traffic
	(kilometers)	(percent)	
United States	187,691	37	0.4
Former Soviet Union	147,359	79	45
India	61,976	51	41[1]
China	54,083	80[2]	56
France	33,446	24	9
Former West Germany	27,028	22	6
Japan	24,412	5	31
United Kingdom	16,896	7	5
Italy	16,138	11	6
Czechoslovakia[3]	13,115	78	30
Switzerland	5,108	40	13
Netherlands	2,780	3	5

[1] 1987
[2] percent of inland freight
[3] Czech Republic plus Slovakia

SOURCES: Length of rail network from U.N. Economic Commission for Europe, Annual Bulletin of Transport Statistics for Europe (Geneva: 1993), International Road Federation, World Road Statistics 1992 (Washington, D.C.: 1992), and Chris Bushell, ed., Jane's Urban Transport Systems 1993-94 (Alexandria, Virginia: Jane's Information Group, Inc., 1993); percentages of passenger and freight traffic are Worldwatch estimates based on the above sources and International Civil Aviation Organization, Traffic: Commercial Air Carriers, 1986-1990, Digest of Statistics, No. 379 (Montreal: 1991), and ICAO, ICAO Statistical Yearbook: Civil Aviation Statistics of the World 1992 (Montreal, 1993).

Eastern Europe now seem eager to gear up for more road transportation. Nearly all railways in Eastern Europe lost passengers along with their old governments; ridership in each country decreased on average nearly 14 percent between 1989 and 1990. Popular sentiment toward public transport is tainted by a tendency to associate it with the despised former regimes. And East Europeans are clamoring to own cars, the icon of success in the West. The *Financial Times* reported in 1991 that twice as many cars were sold in unified Germany as in West Germany the previous year—even though unification increased population only 30 percent.[42]

Eastern Europe and the former Soviet Union retain a substantial urban rail infrastructure, however, including several large metros and more than half the world's 339 light rail and tramway systems. Like the intercity railways, urban networks will be a considerable asset to the region if they survive the current stampede toward private car use. Early, hopeful signs include new equipment and line extensions in 24 cities in the former East Germany, along with rehabilitated train stations in Berlin, Dresden, Leipzig, and Magdeburg. Poland is replacing run-down trains with modern intercity express rail linking Warsaw with Berlin and Vienna; Prague is renovating and expanding its already huge Hlavni Nadrazi station.[43]

The region could further benefit from keeping freight on the rails: Interruptions in goods distribution are among these countries' most serious problems in this time of economic and political transition, and neither the national transport ministries nor the environment can afford a massive buildup of highways. By the end of the decade, East-West European trade could soar as much as tenfold, predicts Georgios Anastassopoulos, vice president of the European Parliament. He warns, "There is a risk that economic growth in Eastern and Central Europe will be crowded out by traffic congestion."[44]

Japan is notable for maintaining high train ridership even as car ownership and use has become widespread; the two-to-one ratio of passenger-kilometers traveled by road versus rail is by far the lowest of any industrial country. (See Table 3.) During the seventies, the government invested roughly 0.6 percent of GDP annually in rail. But in the late eighties, when Japan began privatizing the national network—breaking it up into six regional rail companies and one national freight carrier—investment in rail dropped to between 0.1 and 0.3 percent of GDP.[45]

While many Japanese travel by train, use of rail for freight is

TABLE 3.

Road Versus Rail Travel, Selected Countries, 1991-1992

Country	Road Travel[1]	Rail Travel	Road to Rail Ratio
	(kilometers per person per year)		(road kms per each rail km)
United States	19,141	84	228
Canada[2]	5,480	72	76
United Kingdom	9,827	709	14
Former West Germany	7,675	568	13
Netherlands	10,000	791	13
Denmark	10,577	942	11
Italy	9,105	814	11
Spain	3,718	384	10
France	10,454	1,256	8
Japan	6,115	3,117	2
Poland[3]	1,450	1,091	1
Czechoslovakia[3]	148	1,219	0.1
Former Soviet Union[2]	175	1,403	0.1

[1]Road travel includes private vehicles only
[2]late eighties
[3]Road data include public transport vehicles only

SOURCES: International Road Federation, <u>World Road Statistics 1992</u>
(Washington, D.C.: 1992), U.N. Economic Commission for Europe, <u>Annual Bulletin of Transport Statistics for Europe</u> (Geneva: 1993), and "Riding Rails and Roads," <u>World Monitor</u>, April 1991.

surprisingly low. Trucks carry 90 percent of all goods, an excess that is now backfiring. Costly delays caused by road congestion are undermining Japan's famed "just-in-time" delivery system, in which carefully scheduled trucks make continuous, small deliveries so that industrial and commercial enterprises can avoid keeping large inventories on site. Ironically, this just-in-time delivery system—which auto industry analysts have cred-

ited for Japan's efficiency in car manufacturing—further con-
tributes to traffic congestion, threatening to choke off road
capacity for the industry's own products.[46]

Developing countries, with the notable exceptions of China
and India, have some of the least extensive rail systems in the
world. Many countries have marginal rail service at best, initi-
ated long ago by colonial governments but not adequately
maintained since independence.

China and India, however, have large national rail networks.
China rivals the former Soviet Union in transporting 80 percent
of its inland freight by rail; 56 percent of intercity passenger travel is by train—a greater proportion than in any other country.
Even in China, though, the role of rail
has slipped in favor of increased **Japan is notable**
emphasis on roads. By the end of the **for maintaining**
eighties, China was spending less than **high train**
0.6 percent of GDP on rail, down from
0.9 percent mid-decade. But in **ridership even as**
response to worsening freight bottle- **cars have become**
necks and chronically overcrowded **widespread.**
passenger trains, China intends to par-
ticipate in the global rail revival and invest some $20 billion in
upgrading and expanding railroads by 1995.[47]

India's rail passenger traffic has risen more than fourfold
since 1950. In contrast to other parts of the national infrastructure, the rail system remains reliable and well-maintained,
although much of its equipment dates from the sixties. Both
passenger and freight demand on India's railways are expected
to swell by more than 150 percent during the nineties. Freight
traffic on the rails has grown fivefold in the past four decades,
but trucking is increasing so fast that the share of goods moved
by train is actually waning. In 1992, railways there carried 51
percent of freight, down from 89 percent in 1950.[48]

Large cities in much of Latin America and Asia rely on rail for
public transport. In some cases, suburban rail is a popular
option. In Greater Calcutta, for instance, 1.7 million passengers
a day use suburban rail—compared with roughly 300,000 in
New York and 700,000 in London. In Bombay, suburban rail

accounts for about half of all travel by public transport.[49]

Urban rail is far less common in Africa. Typically, public transport there consists of buses, taxis, and informal public transport vehicles run by private operators. Other than Cairo and Tunis, which have modern rail systems, most cities' local rail service is limited to suburban lines that form part of the national railways.

Reinventing the Rails

Passenger rail seems poised to make a comeback in much of the world. Not only are the rails being revived, they are also being reinvented—with new, sophisticated technologies and advances in comfort and speed. Sleek, quiet versions of old-time trolleys are gliding past stalled motor traffic in cities from Milan to Manila. On long-neglected or abandoned commuter lines to Boston, London, and São Paulo, trains are running once again, now filled with office workers weary of suburban traffic jams. By the end of the decade, passengers in Australia, China, and Taiwan—like people in Japan and Europe today—will ride new high-speed trains between cities in less time than it takes by plane.

It is not surprising that light rail is particularly popular. Light rail is essentially a smoother, quieter version of the nostalgic trolley. Smaller and lighter than rapid rail (metro) cars, light rail cars are also about 20 percent less expensive to build. Unlike rapid rail, light rail does not require an exclusive, separate right-of-way: It can run down the middle or side of a road or in auto-free malls, utility corridors, or even back alleys. This flexibility reduces construction costs by avoiding the need for expensive and time-consuming underground tunnels and elevated tracks. Light rail construction can cost as little as $10-15 million per kilometer, on average one-fifth to one-third as much as a surface metro and one-tenth the cost of an underground subway.[50]

Ironically, several countries that dismantled their trolley systems decades ago to make way for cars are now adopting light rail to ease the resulting smog and traffic jams. Canada, France, the United Kingdom, and the United States are all joining in the light rail revival. Systems are running in five British cities, under construction in two others, and being considered in several additional cities and towns. In the United States, 21 cities have light rail systems and 3 more are planning or building them. In 1990, Los Angeles—once criss-crossed by more than 1,600 kilometers of streetcar tracks—opened its first new light rail line. Much of it uses the abandoned trolley right-of-way. Initially expected to attract 10,000 passengers per day, the line drew 35,000 daily riders in its first year.[51]

In countries where trolleys survived the early automobile boom, some cities have maintained and improved old networks. Japan currently has systems in 19 cities, although Tokyo, which once had 41 streetcar lines, has phased out all but one. Many cities in Western Europe gradually improved their old tram systems after World War II. Typically, streetcar lines were upgraded and relocated in several stages, eventually becoming modern light rail. Today, half of Western Europe's cities with 600,000 or more people have light rail. Germany has 51 light rail networks and, in the eastern part of the country, four old-style tram systems.[52]

Several large cities in the developing world are finding light rail the most appropriate transport investment given their particular conditions—the need to move a large number of people, but little time for construction, very limited funds, and a small amount of available space. Many cities are either building light rail networks or integrating the technologies with traditional rapid rail systems.

Light rail has been proposed for Abidjan, Côte d'Ivoire; Casablanca and Rabat in Morocco; and Johannesburg, South Africa. Mexico has light rail systems in Guadalajara, Mexico City, and Monterrey. Three Brazilian cities have light rail, and in five others it is either authorized or under construction. Manila's 9-year-old light rail line is so popular—whisking people 22 kilometers in 15 minutes while the same stretch by highway can take 2 hours—that the city is planning to start building a second line in 1994. With new shopping centers at 14 of its 15 stations, the added line is expected to spur economic development and cut travel time (compared with driving) 75 percent.[53]

Where governments lack the funds even for the least expensive light rail systems, a promising approach is to refurbish suburban rail and link it to express busways. Dakar, Senegal, and Lagos, Nigeria, have resuscitated suburban rail systems on existing tracks. In both cases, ridership has increased and the systems are now recovering their operating costs—an unusual achievement for any public transport enterprise.[54]

The revival of suburban rail lines in much of the world stems from the need for commuter routes from outlying areas. Whether affluent suburbs or sprawling shantytowns, these peripheral communities are gaining both residents and jobs faster than urban cores. In the United States, for instance, suburban populations are growing at roughly twice the rate of central cities. Even though the central city is usually the single most common destination for commuters, a growing number of urban work trips worldwide bypass city centers. Ring roads, originally meant to speed people around central cities, are now becoming clogged suburb-to-suburb routes.[55]

During the eighties, many cities responded to these trends by investing in commuter rail service—upgrading, expanding, and electrifying existing regional rail lines instead of building more expensive new ones. Some 50 large cities undertook commuter rail projects, including Bombay, Cairo, Chicago, Jakarta, Melbourne, Montreal, and Paris. In the London area, where abandoned crosstown lines reopened and existing commuter rail was upgraded, ridership increased three percent a year in the latter half of the decade, and the system began operating at a profit. Rio de Janeiro and São Paulo revamped their extensive but run-down suburban rail networks, enabling each to handle more than a million passengers daily.[56]

Until recently, commuter rail in the United States was important only in a few old metropolitan areas such as New York, Philadelphia, and San Francisco. In fact, the New York City region alone accounts for 60 percent of the nation's 1.1 million daily commuter rail passengers. But since 1989, nine additional major urban areas, from Miami to Seattle, have planned, begun constructing, or opened commuter rail services. Miami's trains started as a temporary link to West Palm Beach during a highway construction project in 1989, but ridership was so high—1.6 million passengers annually—that transport officials decided to expand the service and make it permanent.[57]

The most ambitious commuter rail revival is in car-dependent Southern California, which recently committed itself to a new 650-kilometer system combining commuter rail with at least 125 kilometers of subway and light rail. Much of it will operate on existing tracks owned by freight railroads. Considered the largest public works project underway in the United States, the completed Southern California system will be second among U.S. rail networks, only to New York's. More than 80 percent of the funding for the project is slated to come from state and local sources, including taxes approved by referendum in 1980 and 1990.[58]

Airlines in Europe are now lobbying for more rail in order to free overloaded terminals of short-trip passengers.

Even more powerful than the renewed enthusiasm for trolleys and commuter rail is popular interest in high-speed passenger rail. Conventional high-speed rail—distinguished from regular rail by aerodynamic railcars and powerful electric motors—has been in successful operation since Japan introduced the Shinkansen or "bullet train" in 1964. The 200 kilometer-per-hour train was completed just in time for the Tokyo Olympics and nearly attracted more attention than the games. Daily ridership on the first line, from Tokyo to Osaka, tripled annually for the first five years. Eventually operating on 4 lines, the bullet trains transported 135 million passengers a year by the late eighties. In 1994, the now private railway companies will begin testing new bullet trains that reach 350 kilometers per hour, compared with the current top speed of 270.[59]

In 1981, France launched its first high-speed rail line, the TGV (Train À Grande Vitesse) from Paris to Lyon. The second line, from Paris to Le Mans on the the country's west coast, is the world's fastest train, reaching more than 300 kilometers an hour on regular runs and a recent trial speed of 515 kilometers per hour. (For comparison, the top speed of a conventional passenger train is roughly 130 kilometers per hour.) The government plans to expand its TGV network to 4,700 kilometers, at a cost of $35 billion, by 2010.[60]

High-speed rail has several clear advantages over highway and air transport, and, if implemented along with adequate investments in regular train service, can provide a useful complement to intercity rail networks. Many high-speed train trips are fast enough to compete with air travel—especially since they save extra time by delivering passengers directly downtown instead of to an airport. The trains are considered ideal for distances of 200 to 1,000 kilometers. The bullet train has almost completely displaced air travel between Nagoya and Tokyo. During the first 10 years of TGV service between Paris and Lyon, the number of rail passengers on that route increased 75 percent, while air travel between the two cities fell by 48 percent. Interestingly, a few airlines in Europe are now lobbying for more rail in order to free overloaded terminals of short-trip passengers. Airlines in Germany, Italy, and Switzerland have begun integrating with railways or even operating their own trains between several large cities and airports.[61]

Despite their great velocity, high-speed trains in France and Japan have never had a passenger fatality in carrying more than 3 billion passengers to date. Another advantage is proven profitability: Although building new high-speed rail lines is relatively expensive (averaging in the range of $3.3 million per kilometer in favorable topography and $20 million per kilometer in rugged terrain), these costs can be recovered with sufficient ridership. Most of the Japanese bullet trains have been profitable for many years, as has the TGV.[62]

Some high-speed trains, including the one employed by the French TGV, can operate on conventional tracks; such versatility enables the fast trains to mesh with existing intercity rail networks. The U.S. plan for adopting high-speed rail relies almost exclusively on upgrading present rail infrastructure on key routes instead of building new rights-of-way. This cost-effective approach can raise speeds considerably while avoiding the pos-

TABLE 4.
Status of High Speed Rail in Selected Countries

Country	First Year of Operation	First Line Opened	Current Top Speed[1]
			—km per hour—
Existing			
Japan	1964	Tokyo-Osaka	270
France	1981	Paris-Lyon	304
Italy	1988	Milan-Rome	250
United States	1988	Washington-New York	200
Germany	1991	Hamburg-Munich	300
Great Britain	1991	London-Newcastle	225
Spain	1992	Madrid-Seville	250
Sweden	1993	Stockholm-Malmö-Gothenburg	200
Planned			
China	1995	Fuzhou-Xiamen	160
Taiwan	1996	Taipei-Kaohsiung	n.a.
Australia	1997	Sydney-Melbourne	350
United States	1998	Houston-Dallas	322
South Korea	2002	Seoul-Pusan	240[2]

[1]Expected speed for planned systems
[2]Average speed
Other future projects include a Rio de Janeiro-São Paolo line in Brazil; Montreal-Windsor line in Canada; Moscow-St. Petersburg in Russia; and Istanbul-Ankara in Turkey.

SOURCE: Worldwatch Institute, based on sources cited in note 64.

sible environmental problems of building new routes. (New high-speed routes cannot simply detour around farmland or environmentally sensitive areas as conventional rail can, because the fastest trains require straight tracks.) In 1993, Amtrak passengers participated in test runs that reached 240 kilometers per hour on regular tracks, thanks to special ultra-fast trains imported from Germany and Sweden.[63]

High-speed rail is now operating in seven countries, most of them in Western Europe. Germany intends to expand its network to some 2,400 kilometers by 2005, and Italy and Spain are each building more than 1,100 kilometers. New lines are being created or planned between major cities in several other countries, including Australia, Brazil, China, Korea, and the United States. (See Table 4). Most of the systems are established incrementally, by first upgrading existing tracks or vehicles and then introducing special high-speed technologies. Record speeds such as the TGV's are reached only by combining high-speed vehicles with high-speed tracks.[64]

European governments are planning to build a vast high-speed rail network that connects such distant corners as Scandinavia, Eastern Europe, the Baltic states, and the Iberian Peninsula, while a version of the TGV will link Britain via the new Channel Tunnel. The scheme aims to put 7,400 kilometers of high-speed rail in place by the end of the nineties, and a total of 20,000 kilometers by 2020. Part of the impetus for the project is the specter of a 74-percent increase in air travel expected to result from Europe's becoming a single market. Governments are counting on high-speed trains to relieve congestion at major European airports, 30 of which are expected to reach full capacity by the year 2000.[65]

A second type of high-speed rail—magnetic levitation trains, which "fly" on a magnetic cushion a few centimeters above a guideway—are still under development. Germany and Japan each have invested roughly $1 billion during the past 20 years in researching "maglev" technology, but so far no passenger service is operating. In March 1994, the German cabinet approved construction of the world's first commercial maglev line. If passed by parliament, the $5-billion project will link Berlin and Hamburg, cutting the 3 1/2-hour journey between the cities to less than 1 hour.[66]

Building the guideways and infrastructure for maglev costs $5 million to $39 million per kilometer, according to available estimates. Doubts about economic feasibility have held back maglev, particularly in the United States: Several private maglev initiatives are suffering from repeated delays because of difficulties in arranging financing. After $725 million for maglev research was inserted in a six-year, national transportation bill in 1991, Congress approved only a fraction of the slated funding in ensuing years, and the President's 1995 budget proposal omitted the program entirely. Safety concerns came to the fore in 1991 when a Japanese maglev caught fire and burned to the ground in a test run. Because of high cost, unresolved safety issues, and the possibility that electromagnetic fields will threaten the health of passengers, wide application of maglev technology seems unlikely for the foreseeable future.[67]

Although the potential benefits of high-speed rail have been amply demonstrated, the effect of high-speed trains on a country's overall transportation network depends on a variety of factors. Researchers warn that although high-speed rail will displace some traffic from highways and airports, it may also create a whole new category of travel. Experience in Europe suggests that many high-speed rail passengers have either switched over from conventional rail—which uses one-fourth to one-half as much energy—or are simply making trips they would not otherwise make. Since the overwhelming majority of car travel consists of relatively short trips, high-speed rail will not substitute for driving as do intercity rail, commuter rail, light rail, and subways. And even where high-speed rail replaces short flights, the airlines will most likely use the freed-up slots to expand their lucrative long distance service—possibly wiping out gains the trains make toward reducing energy use and congestion.[68]

The benefits of high-speed rail can be maximized only if the high-speed system does not divert investment away from a country's basic rail service. In France and Germany, regular rail services on which people have long depended have been reduced recently, and some lines have closed. Critics contend that the new trains create "hypermobility" for the relatively wealthy while stranding those who cannot afford high fares. European transport analyst Jonathon Bray also warns that "if rail investment is skewed too far towards high-speed rail, getting between cities can be quicker than getting across them."[69]

Echoing concern that local rail networks not be neglected, U.K. transport researcher John Whitelegg and his co-editors note in a recent report that high-speed trains have already achieved much by generating long-overdue support for rail travel. But, they conclude, "It remains to be seen whether or not high-speed trains will produce a major revival of rail transport or add their contribution to the extermination of rail as a publicly supported and integrated transport option."[70]

Cars or Trains: A Closer Look At Costs

After decades of traffic congestion, steep oil bills, and smog, many governments are realizing that it was a mistake to abandon railways for highways. Slowly, transport priorities are shifting toward an integrated mix of options instead of overwhelming reliance on motor vehicles. But creating healthy transport systems will require policymakers to make a far greater commitment to improving and expanding rail networks.

When confronted with reversing a trend that has been in motion for most of this century, policymakers cannot help but ask some difficult questions. The foremost is, inevitably, Where will the money come from? Fiscal constraints are universal, with even the strongest national economies now buckling under the strain of a global recession. Adequate funding is hard to come by for all infrastructure, rail included. A second question decision makers face is, How can we ensure that investments in rail will pay off? They commonly fear that new rail service will not attract enough riders. In too many cases, failure to support rail projects with other sensible policies has turned this worry into a self-fulfilling prophecy.

Fortunately, these policy questions do have workable answers. For funding sources, an analysis of most countries' transport sectors reveals vast potential for freeing up funds—by reducing the billions of dollars in hidden subsidies that currently go to other transport modes, particularly highways.

Contrary to popular belief, car drivers do not pay their own way through user fees, but are heavily subsidized. A number of recent studies of driving attempt to separate "internal" costs—which the driver pays—from "external" costs—those borne by others or society at large. The studies agree that external, hidden costs soar so high that driving remains extremely underpriced. Drivers in the United States, for instance, are often surprised to learn that gasoline taxes, vehicle taxes, and road tolls typically cover less than two-thirds the total capital and operating costs of highways. These costs include what all levels of government spend on administration, traffic services, and interest and debt retirement. The amount not covered by user fees—in 1992, more than $32 billion—comes from local property taxes, general fund appropriations and other sources. (See Table 5.)[71]

But direct government expenditures on U.S. automobile travel pale in comparison to the external social costs of driving. Expenses not covered by U.S. drivers include the real value of "free" parking, which may total more than $85 billion per year. Together with other major costs—including those from smog, accidents, and traffic jams—the total U.S. subsidy paid to drivers is estimated to range from $300 - $600 billion per year.[72]

The total U.S. subsidy paid to drivers is estimated to range from $300 - $600 billion per year.

Research in Europe on some of these transport-related costs also reveals sizable hidden subsidies to road and air transport. According to a recent study by the Brussels-based European Federation for Transport and Environment, the externalized social costs of air pollution, carbon emissions, noise, and accidents for every passenger-kilometer of car travel far exceed those not only for train travel but for air travel as well. Driving in Germany involved nearly twice the external costs of air travel—and seven times that of trains. Results were roughly similar in 10 other European countries. (See Table 6.)[73]

Obviously, when these social costs and the external market costs of infrastructure and services are considered, drivers pay only a fraction of the total expense of driving. Although most analysts agree that making drivers fully pay their way would be politically difficult, to say the least, many maintain that the price of car travel should be raised considerably, to reflect more closely the real cost of driving.

TABLE 5.
Funding Sources for U.S. Highway Spending, 1992

	Federal Government	State&Local Governments	TOTAL
	—($US millions)—		
SOURCES[1]			
Highway-user fees (fuel taxes, vehicle taxes, and road tolls)	15,661	36,187	51,848
General fund appropriations, property taxes, and other taxes and fees	1,247	18,344	19,591
Bond issue proceeds	—	9,865	9,865
Investment income and other receipts	908	5,536	6,444
Total funds available[2]	17,816	69,932	84,341
SPENDING[3]			
Capital outlays	220	38,488	38,708
Maintenance and Traffic services	74	22,804	22,878
Other services (administration, research, law enforcement and safety)	430	14,378	14,808
Interest and debt retirement	—	7,947	7,947
Grand Total	724	83,617	84,341

[1]Receipts by collecting agencies. [2]Grand total receipts were $87,748; "total funds available" excludes $3,407 in funds drawn from or placed in reserves.
[3]Disbursements by expending agencies

SOURCE: U.S. Federal Highway Administration, *Highway Statistics 1992* (Washington, D.C.: 1993).

TABLE 6.

Germany: Estimated External Costs of Passenger Transport, 1993

Category	Train	Aircraft	Automobile
	($US per thousand passenger-kilometers)		
Air pollution	1.05	8.54	17.08
Carbon dioxide	2.57	10.76	5.26
Noise	0.35	1.87	1.40
Accidents	1.64	0.23	16.03
Total[1]	5.50	21.41	39.78

[1]Columns may not add to totals due to rounding.

SOURCE: Per Kågeson, *Getting The Prices Right: A European Scheme for Making Transport Pay its True Costs* (Stockholm: European Federation for Transport and Environment, 1993).

The most common, and perhaps most effective, way to internalize the costs of driving is to raise fuel taxes. Low gas taxes contribute to the illusion that using a car is virtually free after the fixed costs of owning an automobile—such as insurance, registration fees, and financing—are paid. Since filling the tank is the expense motorists see most directly, a gas tax can help determine how much people drive. The magnitude of driving-related external costs suggests that even relatively hefty gas taxes in Europe—roughly $0.26 - 0.66 per liter ($1-2.50 per gallon)—do not adequately reflect the cost of driving. It goes without saying that the recent increase in the U.S. federal gas tax to 18 cents a gallon is insufficient.[74]

Another priority is to internalize the costs of parking. Free parking at the workplace, for instance, seems an almost irresistible lure for solo commuting. One effective policy cure is to require employers who provide free parking to offer the alternative of a travel allowance worth the value of the parking space. People who choose the less expensive options of walking, riding bicycles, or using public transport can pocket most of the allotted amount. The County of Los Angeles has successfully used this strategy to reduce its employees' incentive to drive. In 1990, when the county substituted travel allowances for free parking, so many employees stopped driving to work that demand for parking dropped 40 percent. As of 1993, California state law requires companies with 50 or more employees in areas that violate air-quality standards to offer cash instead of subsidized parking.[75]

For internalizing the costs of traffic jams, simple road tolls can be turned into "congestion pricing" programs, which charge a higher fee in congested areas and peak periods to reflect each driver's contribution to delays. Singapore has used a successful congestion pricing scheme since 1975, and officials are planning or considering such systems in Chile, France, Norway, the United Kingdom, the United States, and several other countries. Clifford Winston, senior fellow at the Brookings Institution in Washington, D.C., believes that congestion pricing would help push U.S. drivers out of their cars. He cites a 1983 study in San Francisco that found that congestion tolls would cause a 10 to 20 percent rise in public transit use among downtown commuters.[76]

Unlike fuel taxes and parking fees, however, congestion tolls might merely push some drivers onto other roads. When U.K. researchers recently developed a computer model to evaluate the potential impacts of road pricing on car travel, they found mixed results: While some drivers shifted to public transport, others just drove farther to avoid tolls. In the long run, then, increasing the price of fuel and parking is probably preferable, since road pricing schemes could actually encourage car-dependent sprawl as people shift their activities away from congested areas—where public transport is most often available—to new locations that lack alternatives to driving.[77]

The idea of increasing the price of driving raises concerns that higher fees would disproportionately hurt the poor and the middle class. Although it would be important to offset any regressive effects—for example, through refunds to low-income drivers or cuts in income taxes—it remains unclear whether higher gas taxes and parking fees would be unfairly borne by the less wealthy. Recent research suggests that the external costs of driving itself currently amount to a huge regressive subsidy, accruing disproportionately to wealthy households and paid in part by people who can afford relatively little driving, or none at all.[78]

Making heavy trucks pay for the road damage they inflict would raise additional funds. According to the U.S. General Accounting Office, one 40-ton truck causes as much wear and tear as 9,600 automobiles. Heavy trucks are believed to do 95 percent of all damage to highways in the United States. This imbalance not only drains government funds and causes damage to other vehicles, it also represents an unfair advantage to truck freight over rail freight: Railroads do pay the full costs of maintaining their own infrastructure. Policymakers could level the playing field and recover costs with an annual charge on trucks based on weight and mileage driven. Eight states have weight-distance taxes, as do several West European countries, including Austria, Norway, Portugal, and Sweden.[79]

Heavy trucks are believed to do 95 percent of all damage to highways in the United States.

The eventual impact of reducing road subsidies through increased user fees depends on what is done with the resulting revenue. Typically, funds raised through fuel taxes and tolls are put back into highway spending—a cycle that reinforces the dominance of road transport. One way to address this imbalance—and perhaps make increased user fees more politically palatable—is to return some of the revenue directly to the public as a general tax cut. Another portion of the revenue would also be well spent on expanding and improving railways. A major reason that Western Europe has maintained a relatively high degree of balance among transport modes is that governments historically have allocated only a portion of user fee revenues back to highways. Today, most European countries put about 33 percent of fuel tax revenues into highways; the rest goes into the general fund to support intercity rail, urban public transport, and other transportation options as well as non-transport government programs. Doing so benefits both drivers and nondrivers by providing transport options. And drivers may well gain more in saved time and convenience from reduced congestion than they pay in fuel taxes.[80]

Alternatively, establishment of a national rail trust fund would guarantee funding for rail networks. In the United States, for example, rail is completely shut out of the federal system of trust funds for highways, aviation, and inland waterways. Although gas taxes typically go to the highway fund, airport user fees to the aviation fund, and so forth, correcting a gross imbalance justifies permitting transfers from one fund to another. The U.S. transport system could benefit from such a move: Amtrak needs financial support to upgrade its equipment and expand service to meet rapidly climbing demand. In 1992, Congress considered a legislative proposal to transfer 1 cent per gallon from the federal gas tax—roughly $1 billion per year—into a trust fund for passenger rail capital improvements. Another proposal in 1993 suggested creating such a fund by switching roughly $30 million each year from the diesel fuel taxes paid by Amtrak and the freight railroads into a rail trust fund.[81]

Partial privatization is another funding option for rail. A totally privatized market cannot be trusted to offer service on vital but unprofitable routes. Especially since rail must compete with far more flexible highway transport, it is crucial for railways to be as comprehensive as possible. The social value lost when a network is disrupted by reducing rail service often far outweighs the economic gains an operator may realize.

A wide range of private participation can help governments offset the costs of rail service. For instance, private companies can invest capital in a publicly owned railway. In the state of São Paulo, Brazil, private investments are helping the state-owned railroad build intermodal cargo terminals, enabling rail to compete better with truck freight. In addition to supplementing public funds for financing, building, and operating rail projects, the private sector can be tapped for managerial, marketing, and technical skills. Public rail entities can also contract with independent operators to provide passenger rail service—an approach that works best if the operators are required to maintain certain standards of safety, quality, and, on less heavily used lines, guaranteed service.[82]

The impressive return on investment in rail is easily demonstrated if environmental and social criteria are incorporated. Rail's worth to society extends far beyond mere farebox revenues. Public transport services that cover their own costs through passenger fares are extremely rare (San Diego's popular trolley is one recent exception, repaying 92 percent of operating costs through fares). But having rail as an alternative to driving represents an incalculable societal gain, avoiding the high costs of pollution, traffic congestion, oil dependence, and road accidents. The European Conference of Ministers of Transport estimates that the financial return on investment in highways now being built in France is 10 percent and the social return (putting a dollar value on time saved and convenience) 20 percent. Similar estimates for the TGV—France's two high-speed rail lines—are a financial return of 12-17 percent and a social return of 20-33 percent.[83]

Most European countries put about two-thirds of fuel tax revenues into the general fund—to support intercity rail and urban public transport, among other programs.

In addition, economists generally agree that infrastructure improvements are a sound investment. More specifically, a recent U.S. study looked at the impact of government transport expenditures on worker productivity. A 10-year, $100-billion increase in public transport spending was estimated to boost worker output by $521 billion—compared with $237 billion for the same level of spending on highways. Moreover, public transport investments began returning net benefits nearly three times as quickly as highway expenditures.[84]

Other research has drawn similar conclusions. In a 1991 study, the Washington, D.C.-based Urban Institute and Boston-based Cambridge Systematics compared the economic effects of investing in rehabilitation and continued operation of SEPTA (the light rail, subway, and commuter rail system in the Philadelphia metropolitan area) with cutting or eliminating its services. The study found that for every dollar of public spending on rebuilding and operating SEPTA, $3 would accrue to the state and the region as a direct result of improved transport. The total economic impact, including increases in business sales, jobs, personal income, population, and the accompanying rise in state and local tax revenues, would be nine dollars for every dollar invested.[85]

Keeping the Revival On Track

Now that much of the world has rediscovered trains, it is time to speed up the global revival, and to reap the environmental, social, and economic rewards of riding the rails. With a growing number of governments stepping up funding, rail travel is likely to fare much better in the twenty-first century than it did in most of the twentieth. For governments to maximize the financial return on their investments, though, rail services need to run at full capacity. Encouraging the needed switch from cars to trains will require supportive policies.

One way to ensure that people will use a rail system is to integrate it thoroughly with other transport modes. In cities, even the most comprehensive rail network cannot reach every neighborhood. Convenient links with suburban bus routes can make the system work for a large number of riders. Similarly, more passengers can use intercity trains if rail lines coordinate with bus service so that out-of-town travelers can easily reach their final destination. Transport planners would be wise to avoid repeating a mistake often made in U.S. cities—failure to provide direct rail service to airports.

Attracting as many riders as possible also requires easy access to rail stations. Many rail authorities concentrate solely on providing car parking—a strategy severely restricted by the expense and limited availability of land. An often overlooked alternative is to provide safe bicycle parking and to design stations so that pedestrians can approach the entrances easily. Making it convenient for people to walk or cycle to the station frees up car parking space and accommodates nondrivers. Commuter rail can get an extra boost in ridership by allowing bicycles onto trains; this enables riders to reach the rail system from either the home or the workplace, even if neither one is within walking distance of a station.[86]

"Bike-and-ride" is exceptionally popular in Japan and much of Europe. In Denmark, 25 to 30 percent of commuter rail passengers begin their trip from home on a bicycle. In the Netherlands, bicycling is officially considered the most important means of transport to rail stations.[87]

For the long term, the most far-reaching way to encourage widespread use of rail is to promote compact land use in cities, suburbs, and towns. No amount of investment in rail can overcome automobile dependence in a region marked by sprawl. Although planning future urban growth is best left to local authorities and citizens, national governments can use compact land-use criteria as a condition for funding local and regional transport projects.

To qualify for national funds, for example, a local rail project (or any other major transport improvement) would have to be accompanied by measures to ensure compact growth. Zoning codes could steer high-density development to the area around rail stations and along rail lines. Developers can be given incentives to site housing, shops, and offices in key areas. Perhaps most important, rail planners would be required to collaborate closely with the region's land use planners in designing the entire system.

Several large cities have used this approach, turning urban growth to their advantage by investing in rail networks and deliberately concentrating further development along the rail lines. In Paris, Hamburg, Stockholm, and Toronto, rail corridors have helped induce compact, efficient land use. These areas depend far less on automobiles than other cities—fostering not only increased rail ridership, but more cycling and walking as well. They also have maintained their urban appeal and livability

by using rail lines as a focal point for pedestrian-friendly commercial development and high-density office and residential
areas.[88]

In addition to these strategies for maximizing rail use, governments can amplify economic benefits by encouraging domestic industries to produce rail equipment. This is especially
important for developing countries trying to support a high-
value manufacturing base. Mexico, for instance, has been able
to build most of its own subway cars. And in countries where
most people cannot afford to buy cars, railcar production is
likely to pose fewer economic risks than trying to establish a
domestic automobile industry.[89]

The debt-ridden, capital-short countries of Eastern Europe
and the former Soviet Union already possess a large capacity to
supply rail equipment. The former East Germany has particularly impressive expertise in building railcars, which could be produced for export. Czechoslovakia has a similar opportunity:
The world's largest tram factory is located in a suburb of Prague.
A German-based conglomerate is now investing in the plant,
which was retooled in 1993 and has turned to manufacturing
light rail vehicles, including those for Manila's new light rail
line.[90]

Industrial countries can also benefit from railcar manufacture.
The United States, once a leader in building passenger railcars,
is well-positioned to re-enter the market, employing skilled
workers who lost jobs in declining heavy industries such as steel
production. A long-closed manufacturing plant in the San
Francisco area, for example, has been renovated to turn out the
new "California car," a special double-deck commuter railcar. An
old Pullman freight-car plant in Chicago recently reopened to
produce 173 new railcars and rebuild 140 existing cars for the
Chicago commuter rail authority.[91]

Producing rail equipment can aid economic conversion at
anachronistic Cold War defense plants. In the Rosyth Royal
Dockyard in Scotland, workers who have traditionally maintained the Royal Navy's ships and submarines are currently
overhauling 738 railcars for the London Underground. Although
the dockyard probably will remain largely dependent on defense

work for the immediate future, its success in refurbishing rail equipment hints at the considerable scope for such conversions in the long term.[92]

A global rail revival is under way, kicked off by a series of transport crises including smog and traffic jams. Although the advantages of trains have become more compelling than ever, a lasting shift to greater rail use will come only if governments reform today's lopsided transport policies. The payback promises to be huge. If future rail expansions are supported by policies that remove unfair transport subsidies, integrate various transport modes, and encourage wiser land use—everyone, not just train riders, will benefit.

Notes:

1. The 20-fold increase from William Fulton and Stephen Svete, "Is Metrolink More Than an Insurance Policy Against Disaster?" *Los Angeles Times*, February 13, 1994; Sharon Moeser, "Santa Clarita Train Line to Get 5th Station," *Los Angeles Times*, February 5, 1994; Ralph Frammolino, "The Metrolink Will Never Be the Same," *Los Angeles Times*, January 20, 1994.

2. Scott Armstrong, "Angelenos Can't Shake Auto Habits Even After Earthquake," *Christian Science Monitor*, February 17, 1994.

3. Sweden from Transport and Environmental Studies of London (TEST), *Wrong Side of the Tracks? Impacts of Road and Rail Transport on the Environment* (London: 1991); "Germans to Invest More in Rail than Road," *International Railway Journal*, July 1992; Ferdinand Protzman, "To Track Unity in Europe, Watch Its Fast Trains," *New York Times*, October 25, 1992.

4. Energy comparison, which applies to U.S. commuting conditions, is based on Deborah Gordon, *Steering A New Course: Transportation, Energy, and the Environment* (Washington, D.C.: Island Press, 1991), using average commuting occupancies of 50 passengers for intercity rail and 100 passengers for commercial air; emissions from Campaign for New Transportation Priorities (CNTP), "Get America On Track," Washington, D.C., 1993.

5. U.S. General Accounting Office (GAO), *Smart Highways: An Assessment of Their Potential to Improve Travel* (Washington, D.C.: 1991); "Airway Pollution," *Energy Economist*, January 1994.

6. Japan from "Analysis and Evaluation," in John Whitelegg, Staffan Hultén and Torbjörn Flink, eds., *High Speed Trains: Fast Tracks to the Future* (Hawes, North Yorkshire, U.K.: Leading Edge Press, 1993); U.S. figure represents average fatality rates from the 10-year period ending in 1991, from National Safety Council, *Accident Facts, 1993 Edition* (Itasca, Illinois: 1993).

7. Rail versus highway space from CNTP, "Intercity Passenger Transportation: Neglect of Rail and Intermodal Facilities," CNTP Policy Series Paper No. 5, Washington, D.C., August 1991; O'Hare versus Gare Saint-Lazare from the Organization for Economic Cooperation and Development (OECD), "New Policy Approaches to International Air Transport," discussions from the OECD Forum for the Future conference, Paris, June 29, 1992; CNTP, op. cit. note 4.

8. Atlanta from American Public Transit Association (APTA), "Public Transit Works for America," *Transit California*, monthly publication of the Sacramento-based California Transit Association, November 1993; London and Brussels from Richard Tolmach, "British Discover Stations as Magnets for Development," *Moving People*, bi-monthly publication of the Sacramento-based Modern Transit Society, September-October 1993.

9. Share of world's people who can afford a car from Ed Ayres, "Bicycle Production Resumes Climb," in Lester R. Brown, Hal Kane, and Ed Ayres, *Vital Signs 1993* (New York: W.W.Norton & Co., 1993); Data on car ownership are for 1991, from American Automobile Manufacturers Association (AAMA), *AAMA Motor Vehicle Facts and Figures '93* (Detroit, Mich.: 1993); share of global air travel is from OECD, "International Air Transport 2000: The Challenges of Growth and Competition," (Paris: June 1992); U.S. households figure is for 1990, from U.S. Federal Highway Administration (FHWA), *New Perspectives in Commuting* (Washington, D.C.: July 1992); fear of flying from CNTP, op. cit., note 4.

10. European Conference of Ministers of Transport (ECMT), *Investment in Transport Infrastructure in ECMT Countries* (Paris: 1988); "Clinton Seeks Amtrak Increase," *News from the National Association of Railroad Passengers (NARP)*, monthly newsletter of the Washington, D.C.-based NARP, February 1994.

11. Rail travel as percentage of U.S. intercity travel from sources cited in Table 2; road versus rail travel from sources cited in Table 3.

12. Non-user fee sources of U.S. highway spending from U.S. Federal Highway Administration, *Highway Statistics 1992* (Washington, D.C.: 1993); $300-billion figure from James J. MacKenzie, Roger C. Dower, and Donald D.T. Chen, *The Going Rate: What it Really Costs to Drive* (Washington, D.C.: World Resources Institute, 1992); a range of $380-660 billion is given in Peter Miller and John Moffet, *The Price of Mobility: Uncovering the Hidden Costs of Transportation* (New York: National Resources Defense Council, October 1993).

13. Sources for Table 1 are as follows: Deborah Gordon, op. cit., note 4; CNTP, op. cit., note 4; "Analysis and Evaluation," in Whitelegg et al., op. cit., note 6; American Public Transit Association, op. cit., note 8. Amount of oil potentially displaced in the United States is Worldwatch Institute estimate based on Motor Vehicle Manufacturers Association (MVMA), *Facts and Figures '91* (Detroit, Mich.: 1991), on Stacy C. Davis and Melissa D. Morris, *Transportation Energy Data Book: Edition 12* (Oak Ridge, Tenn.: Oak Ridge National Laboratory, 1992), and on U.S. Department of Energy, Energy Information Administration, *Annual Energy Review 1990* (Washington, D.C.: 1991); potential U.K. carbon reduction is Worldwatch Institute estimate based on TEST, op cit., note 3.

14. TEST, op. cit., note 3.

15. Btu per passenger-kilometer are based on Gordon, op. cit., note 4, using average commuting occupancies of 50 passengers for intercity rail, 100 passengers for commercial air, 50 for urban rail, and 65 for commuter rail. The energy efficiency of urban rail varies widely from system to system.

16. U.S. Federal Railroad Administration, *Rail vs Truck Fuel Efficiency: The Relative Fuel Efficiency of Truck Competitive Rail Freight and Truck Operations Compared in a Range of Corridors* (Washington, D.C.: April 1991); international comparisons from U.S. Congress, Office of Technology Assessment (OTA), *Energy in Developing Countries* (Washington, D.C.: U.S. Government Printing Office, 1991).

17. Mark D. Levine et al., *Energy Efficiency, Developing Nations, and Eastern Europe* (Washington, D.C.: International Institute for Energy Conservation (IIEC), 1991).

18. TEST, op. cit., note 3.

19. Edson L. Tennyson, "Impact on Transit Patronage of Cessation or Inauguration of Rail Service," *Transportation Research Record 1221* (Washington,

D.C.: National Research Council, 1989); Los Angeles study cited in Campaign for New Transportation Priorities (CNTP), "Urban and Suburban Transportation: Programs and Policies for More Livable Cities," CNTP Policy Series Paper No. 1, Washington, D.C., March 1991.

20. TEST, op. cit., note 3.

21. OTA, *Delivering the Goods: Public Works Technologies, Management, and Financing* (Washington, D.C.: U.S. Government Printing Office, 1991); GAO, *Traffic Congestion: Trends, Measures, and Effects* (Washington, D.C.: 1989).

22. Share of U.S. freight that moves by rail is from sources cited in Table 2; Carmichael cited in CNTP, "Intercity Freight Transportation: The Multiple Threats of Bigger, Longer Trucks," CNTP Policy Series Paper No. 4, Washington, D.C., March 1991; ways to increase rail capacity from Frank N. Wilner, "User Charges and Transportation Efficiency," Association of American Railroads, Washington, D.C., 1990.

23. Cost of air traffic congestion from U.S. Department of Transportation, *Moving America: New Directions, New Opportunities* (Washington, D.C.: 1990); Harriet Parcells, "Airport and Highway Expansion on the Line: The Rail Option," presented at Transportation for Sustainable Communities, conference sponsored by the Center for Neighborhood Technology, Chicago, Illinois, December 13, 1991.

24. Parcells, op. cit., note 23; CNTP, op. cit., note 7; cost estimates cited in CNTP, "Get America On Track," Washington, D.C., 1993.

25. CNTP, op. cit., note 7; TEST, op. cit., note 3.

26. London and other Europe examples from Richard Tolmach, op. cit., note 8.

27. Montgomery County Planning Department, *Montgomery County Comprehensive Growth Policy Study* (Silver Spring, Maryland: 1989), cited in Michael Replogle, "Sustainability: A Vital Concept for Transportation Planning and Development," *Journal of Advanced Transportation*, Spring 1991.

28. U.S. figures represent the average from the 10-year period ending in 1991, from National Safety Council, *Accident Facts, 1993 Edition* (Itasca, Illinois: 1993); European figures from European Communities Commission, *Transport Annual Statistics 1970-1989* (Luxembourg: 1991), and from ECMT, "Trends in the Transport Sector 1970-1990," Paris, 1991.

29. British Department of Transport estimate cited in Jonathon Bray, *Transport: Policy Options*, Economic Alternatives for Eastern Europe Briefing No. 5 (London: New Economics Foundation, 1992); TEST, op. cit., note 3; U.S. estimate from The Urban Institute, *The Costs of Highway Crashes* (Washington, D.C.: 1991).

30. ECMT, *Freight Transport and the Environment* (Paris: 1991); Wilner, "User Charges and Transportation Efficiency."

31. David Schwab, "Airport Noise Report is Again Postponed," *The Star-Ledger* (New Jersey), August 27, 1992; TEST, op. cit., note 3. U.S. example from Wilner, op. cit, note 22.

32. Data on car ownership is for 1991, from American Automobile Manufacturers Association (AAMA), *AAMA Motor Vehicle Facts and Figures '93* (Detroit, Mich.: 1993); U.S. households figure is for 1990, from FHWA, op. cit., note 9; estimated share of population physically unable to drive from F.E.K. Britton, "Cars, Transport and Amenity in Urban Places: A Reader" (draft), Paris, 1990.

33. Number of passengers per year from Kenneth T. Jackson, *Crabgrass Frontier, The Suburbanization of the United States* (New York: Oxford University Press, 1985); Gordon, op. cit., note 4; inadequate service provided by traction companies in the early decades of the twentieth century described in Scott L. Bottles, *Los Angeles and the Automobile: The Making of the Modern City* (Berkeley: University of California Press, 1987); transport conspiracy described in Jonathan Kwitny, "The Great Transportation Conspiracy," *Harper's*, February 1981.

34. Percent of intercity travel calculated from sources cited in Table 2; CNTP, op. cit., note 4.

35. 1925 figure from GAO, *Railroad Competitiveness: Federal Laws and Policies Affect Railroad Competitiveness* (Washington, D.C.: 1991); breakdown of U.S. freight transport from Association of American Railroads, *Railroad Facts 1993 Edition* (Washington, D.C.: August 1993); other figures calculated from sources cited in Table 2.

36. Lawrence H. Kaufman, "Truckers Turn to Rails For the Long Haul," *Journal of Commerce*, February 20, 1992; number of intermodal shipments from "The Return of the Railroads?" *The Economist*, November 27, 1993.

37. Nancy Heiser, "Federal Aid to Domestic Transportation: A Brief History from the 1800s to the 1980s," U.S. Congressional Research Service, Washington, D.C., August 1988; 1990 figures from CNTP, op. cit., note 7; Don Phillips, "Budget Favors Transportation," *Washington Post*, January 17, 1994.

38. U.S. Department of Transportation (DOT), *National Transportation Strategic Planning Study* (Washington, D.C.: 1990).

39. Rail's share of freight traffic from ECMT, "Trends in the Transport Sector 1970-1990"; Bruce Barnard, "EC Panel Takes Step to Shift Freight from Roads to Water, Sea and Rails," *Journal of Commerce*, February 20, 1992.

40. John May, "World-Class Destruction," *New York Times*, February 18, 1992; "Swiss Approve Rail Tunnels Under the Alps," *Washington Post*, September 28, 1992; Alan Riding, "Swiss Give New Meaning to the Word Roadblock," *New York Times*, February 28, 1994.

41. OECD countries' investments from ECMT, *Investment in Transport Infrastructure in ECMT Countries* (Paris: 1988); Sweden from TEST, op. cit., note 3. "Germans to Invest More in Rail than Road," *International Railway Journal*, July 1992.

42. United Nations, Economic Commission for Europe (ECE), *Transport Information* (New York: 1991); *Financial Times* article cited in Bray, op. cit., note 29.

43. Number of light rail and tramway systems from Chris Bushell, ed., *Jane's Urban Transport Systems 1993-94* (Alexandria, Virginia: Jane's Information Group, Inc., 1993); recent rail improvements in the region from untitled article, *Moving*

People, August, 1993.

44. Keith Rockwell, "EC Officials Lament Inaction On East Europe's Transit Crisis," *Journal of Commerce*, October 31, 1991.

45. Akiyoshi Yamamoto, Deputy Director, Japan Railways Group/East Japan Railway Company, New York, private communication, April 30, 1992.

46. A.E. Cullison, "Congested Roads in Japan Thwart Just-in-Time Efficiency," *Journal of Commerce*, March 16, 1992.

47. Share of passenger and freight traffic carried by rail calculated from sources cited in Table 2; government spending in eighties from Hennie Deboeck, financial analyst, World Bank, Washington, D.C., private communication, April 22, 1992; Xie Yicheng, "Green Light is Given to Build More Rail Track, *China Daily*, January 13, 1993.

48. Lincoln Kaye, "On the Right Track," *Far Eastern Economic Review*, July 28, 1988; demand projections from "Railways Going Hi-Tech in Every Area," *India Economic News*, October 1991; 1992 freight figure calculated from sources cited in Table 2; 1950 figure from C. Rammanohar Reddy et al., "The Debt-Energy Nexus: A Case Study of India," International Energy Initiative, Bangalore, India, April 1992.

49. All ridership figures from Gerhard Menckhoff, "Urban Transit Options in South Asia," presented at the Mid-Atlantic Region of the Association for Asian Studies 17th Annual Meeting, Indiana University of Pennsylvania, October 21-23, 1988.

50. "A Streetcar Named Light Rail," *IEEE Spectrum*, February 1991; cost figures from Alan Armstrong-Wright, *Urban Transit Systems: Guidelines for Examining Options* (Washington, D.C.: World Bank, 1986).

51. Richard Tomkins, "Manchester's Metrolink: A Testbed for Britain," *Financial Times*, April 6, 1992; number of U.S. cities with light rail from Bushell, op. cit., note 43; length of Los Angeles's former streetcar network from William S. Kowinski, "There's Still Time to Hop a Trolley—Vintage or Modern," *Smithsonian*, February 1988; Karen Zagor, "Light Rail Systems: Revival of Interest in North America," *Financial Times*, April 6, 1992.

52. Bushell, op. cit., note 43; phasing out of streetcar lines in Tokyo from Tokyo Metropolitan Government, *Plain Talk About Tokyo* (Tokyo: January 1991); Tomkins, op. cit., note 51; number of light rail networks in Germany from Bushell, op. cit., note 43.

53. Richard Barrett, Africa Technical Department, Infrastructure Division, World Bank, Washington, D.C., private communication, October 10, 1990; cities in Latin America from Bushell, op. cit., note 43; time savings on Manila's first light rail line from "Breaking Up the Jams," *Asiaweek*, February 28, 1992; new line from Rigoberto Tiglao, "Looking for a New Ride," *Far Eastern Economic Review*, November 4, 1993.

54. Richard Barrett, private communication, op. cit., note 53.

55. DOT, op. cit., note 38.

56. London from Regional Plan Association, *The Renaissance of Rail Transit in America* (New York: 1991); other cities from Chris Bushell and Peter Stonham, eds., *Jane's Urban Transport Systems 1985* (London: Jane's Publishing Company, 1985).

57. Daniel Machalaba, "Longtime Symbols of Decay and Delay, Commuter Railroads Undergo a Revival," *Wall Street Journal*, October 1, 1991; ridership on Miami commuter trains from American Public Transit Association, "Commuter Rail Transport," Washington, D.C., 1991; permanent service for Miami from Matthew L. Wald, "Railroads Are a Growth Industry, for a Change," *New York Times*, June 20, 1993.

58. Private communication, Steve Chesser, spokesperson, Metropolitan Transportation Authority (MTA), Los Angeles, California, March 14, 1994.

59. Joseph Vranich, *Supertrains: Solutions to America's Transportation Gridlock* (New York: St. Martin's Press, 1991); plans for new bullet trains from Bill O'Neill, "Beating the Bullet Train, *New Scientist*, October 2, 1993.

60. Vranich op. cit., note 59; French government's plans for TGV expansion from Walter C. Streeter, "The French Train à Grande Vitesse: Focusing on the TGV-Atlantique," Working Paper 558, Institute of Urban and Regional Development, University of California, Berkeley, March 1992.

61. Michel Guyard, Transportation Counselor, French Embassy, Washington, D.C., private communication, May 18, 1990; travel between Nagoya and Tokyo from Mamoru Taniguchi, "High Speed Rail in Japan: A Review and Evaluation of the Shinkansen Train," Working Paper 557, Institute of Urban and Regional Development, University of California, Berkeley, March 1992. First 10 years of TGV from Mark Reutter, "The Lost Promise of the American Railroad," *Wilson Quarterly*, Winter 1994; Jessica Tuchman Mathews, "Getting Back on Track," *Washington Post*, November 29, 1991; airlines operating rail services from Joseph Vranich, "Aviation Needs High-Speed Rail," *Journal of Commerce*, February 19, 1993.

62. Safety and profitability from Vranich, op. cit., note 59; cost range from DOT, op. cit., note 38.

63. Don Phillips, "High-Speed Eurotrains Race to Win Amtrak Contract for Northeast Route," *Washington Post*, July 25, 1993.

64. New lines in Germany, Italy, and Spain from Richard Tomkins, "Final Search for the Missing Link," *Financial Times*, March 31, 1993; sources for Table 4 are Taniguchi, op. cit., note 61; Francoise Adams, special assistant, French Embassy, Washington, D.C., private communication, May 18, 1990; Vranich, op. cit., note 59; Scott Pendleton, "Bullet-Train Plan Builds Steam," *Christian Science Monitor*, March 3, 1992; Mich Hamer, "The Second Railway Revolution," *New Scientist*, May 23, 1992; P.T. Bangsberg, "Japan to Help Build High-Speed Rail in China," *Journal of Commerce*, May 7, 1992; U.S. DOT, op. cit., note 38; John Ridding, "Korea's High-Speed Train Race Begins," *Financial Times*, December 5, 1990; John Burton, "South Korea Bargains Hard to Take the Fast Train," *Financial Times*, August 23, 1993; John Murray Brown, "Turkey to Revive High-Speed Rail Plan," *Financial Times*, August 5, 1992; and John Ridding and Quentin

Peel, "Next Chapter of the Railway Children," *Financial Times*, November 18, 1993.

65. Mick Hamer, op. cit., note 64; projected increase in air travel from Parcells, op. cit., note 23.

66. Research in Germany and Japan from Gino Del Guercio, "When Even the Local Is an Express," *World Monitor*, December 1992; Quentin Peel, "Go-ahead for Transrapid Rail Plan," *Financial Times*, March 3, 1994.

67. Cost per kilometer from Malcolm W. Browne, "New Funds Fuel Magnet Power for Trains," *New York Times*, March 3, 1992; funding history from Susan Sumner, Vice President, High Speed Rail/Maglev Association, Alexandria, Virginia, private communication, March 2, 1994; fire incident described in Gary Stix, "Riding on Air," *Scientific American*, February 1992.

68. For a thorough discussion of the potential benefits and drawbacks of high-speed rail, see Whitelegg et al., op. cit., note 6.

69. Bray, op. cit., note 29.

70 Whitelegg et al., op.cit., note 6.

71. For a comprehensive overview of the results of several studies, see MacKenzie et al., op. cit., note 12; Miller and Moffet, op. cit., note 12; for an annotated bibliography, see U.S. Federal Railroad Administration, *Environmental Externalities and Social Costs of Transportation Systems—Measurement, Mitigation and Costing* (Washington, D.C.: August 1993). Non-user fees as sources for U.S. highway spending from U.S. FHWA, op. cit., note 12.

72. $300-billion figure from MacKenzie et al., op. cit., note 12; a range of $380-660 billion is given in Miller and Moffet, op. cit., note 12.

73. Per Kågeson, *Getting the Prices Right: A European Scheme for Making Transport Pay its True Costs* (Stockholm: European Federation for Transport and Environment, 1993).

74. Vukan R. Vuchic, "Cheap Gasoline: An American Addiction," *Moving People*, April/May 1993; gas taxes in Europe from ibid.

75. Los Angeles example from Jeffrey Tumlin and Patrick Siegman, "The Cost of Free Parking," *Urban Ecologist*, Summer 1993; see also Donald Shoup, *Cashing Out Employer-Paid Parking* (Washington, D.C.: U.S. DOT, 1992); California law from Mary Catherine Snyder, "Employees Cash In at Work," *The Surface Transportation Policy Project Bulletin*, March 1993.

76. Countries considering congestion pricing from Kenneth A. Small, "Urban Traffic Congestion: A New Approach to the Gordian Knot," *The Brookings Review*, Spring 1993, and from Kiran Bhatt, "Seminar Presentations and Discussions," in FHWA, *Exploring the Role of Pricing as a Congestion Management Tool*, proceedings of the Seminar on the Application of Pricing Principles to Congestion Management, Washington, D.C., July 23, 1991; Clifford Winston, "Efficient Transportation Infrastructure Policy," *Journal of Economic Perspectives*, Winter 1991; 1983 study cited is Philip A. Viton, "Pareto- Optimal Urban Transportation Equilibria," *Research in Transportation Economics*, No. 1, 1983.

77. Computer model described in Charlene Rohr and Mike Salter, "Model Drivers?" *Transport Innovation*, Autumn 1992; land-use implications raised by John Whitelegg, Lancaster University Department of Geography, Lancaster, U.K., private communication, October 11, 1993.

78. Assuming a $1-per-gallon gasoline subsidy and using U.S. data for average annual gasoline expenditures and household income, Kirk R. Barrett has calculated that households in the highest income bracket receive a subsidy of $1,700 per year, compared with $300 per year for households in the lowest income bracket; Kirk R. Barrett, "Increased Gasoline Tax: It's Only Fair," Northwestern University, Evanston, Illinois, unpublished paper, February 1993. See also A. N. Bleijenberg, *Transport, Economy and Environment* (Delft, Netherlands: Center for Energy Conservation and Environmental Technologies, 1992.)

79. Wilner, op. cit., note 22, citing GAO Controller General, *Excessive Truck Weight: An Expensive Burden We Can No Longer Support* (Washington, D.C.: 1979); heavy trucks' share of damage in the United States from MacKenzie et al., op. cit., note 12; CNTP, op. cit., note 22; West European countries from Wilner, op. cit., note 22.

80. Apportionment of European fuel tax revenues from DOT, op. cit., note 38.

81. W. Graham Claytor, Jr., "A Penny for Amtrak," *Washington Post*, April 28, 1992; "Rail Fund Concept Gets First Hearing," *News from the National Association of Railroad Passengers*, August 1993.

82. James Bruce, "Brazilian Privatization Takes New Twist With Train Loan," *Journal of Commerce*, January 28, 1991.

83. San Diego trolley from Regional Plan Association, op. cit., note 56; European Conference of Ministers of Transport (ECMT), *Private and Public Investment in Transport*, Report of the Eighty-First Round Table on Transport Economics (Paris: OECD, 1990).

84. David Alan Aschauer, "Transportation Spending and Economic Growth: The Effects of Transit and Highway Expenditures," American Public Transit Association, Washington, D.C., September 1991.

85. The Urban Institute and Cambridge Systematics, Inc., "Public Transportation Renewal as an Investment: The Economic Impacts of SEPTA on the Regional and State Economy," Delaware Valley Regional Planning Commission, Philadelphia, Pennsylvania, May 1991.

86. For a thorough analysis of the potential for linking bicycle transportation with rail, see Michael Replogle and Harriet Parcells, "Linking Bicycle/Pedestrian Facilities with Transit," report prepared for the U.S. Federal Highway Administration, September 1992, and Michael A. Replogle, *Bicycles and Public Transportation: New Links to Suburban Transit Markets*, 2nd ed. (Washington, D.C.: The Bicycle Federation, 1988).

87. Replogle and Parcells, op. cit., note 86.

88. Peter Newman and Jeffrey Kenworthy, *Cities and Automobile Dependence: An International Sourcebook* (Aldershot, U.K.: Gower, 1989).

89. Mexico example from Mia Layne Birk and Deborah Lynn Bleviss, eds., *Driving New Directions* (Washington, D.C.: IIEC, 1991).

90. *Moving People*, op. cit., note 43; Manila's light railcars from Rigoberto Tiglao, "Looking for a New Ride," op. cit., note 53.

91. San Francisco from Rick Morales, Rail Transportation Associate, Caltrans (California Department of Transportation), Sacramento, private communication, March 3, 1994; Chris Knapton, Director of Media Relations, Metra (commuter rail service for northeast Illinois), private communication, March 2, 1994.

92. Gordon Dabinett, "Tanks into Trams?" *Transport Innovation*, September 1992.

THE WORLDWATCH PAPER SERIES

No. of
Copies

_____ 57. **Nuclear Power: The Market Test** by Christopher Flavin.
_____ 58. **Air Pollution, Acid Rain, and the Future of Forests** by Sandra Postel.
_____ 60. **Soil Erosion: Quiet Crisis in the World Economy** by Lester R. Brown and
        Edward C. Wolf.
_____ 61. **Electricity's Future: The Shift to Efficiency and Small-Scale Power**
        by Christopher Flavin.
_____ 62. **Water: Rethinking Management in an Age of Scarcity** by Sandra Postel.
_____ 63. **Energy Productivity: Key to Environmental Protection and Economic Progress**
        by William U. Chandler.
_____ 65. **Reversing Africa's Decline** by Lester R. Brown and Edward C. Wolf.
_____ 66. **World Oil: Coping With the Dangers of Success** by Christopher Flavin.
_____ 67. **Conserving Water: The Untapped Alternative** by Sandra Postel.
_____ 68. **Banishing Tobacco** by William U. Chandler.
_____ 69. **Decommissioning: Nuclear Power's Missing Link** by Cynthia Pollock.
_____ 70. **Electricity For A Developing World: New Directions** by Christopher Flavin.
_____ 71. **Altering the Earth's Chemistry: Assessing the Risks** by Sandra Postel.
_____ 73. **Beyond the Green Revolution: New Approaches for Third World Agriculture**
        by Edward C. Wolf.
_____ 74. **Our Demographically Divided World** by Lester R. Brown and Jodi L. Jacobson.
_____ 75. **Reassessing Nuclear Power: The Fallout From Chernobyl** by Christopher Flavin.
_____ 76. **Mining Urban Wastes: The Potential for Recycling** by Cynthia Pollock.
_____ 77. **The Future of Urbanization: Facing the Ecological and Economic Constraints**
        by Lester R. Brown and Jodi L. Jacobson.
_____ 78. **On the Brink of Extinction: Conserving The Diversity of Life** by Edward C. Wolf.
_____ 79. **Defusing the Toxics Threat: Controlling Pesticides and Industrial Waste**
        by Sandra Postel.
_____ 80. **Planning the Global Family** by Jodi L. Jacobson.
_____ 81. **Renewable Energy: Today's Contribution, Tomorrow's Promise** by
        Cynthia Pollock Shea.
_____ 82. **Building on Success: The Age of Energy Efficiency** by Christopher Flavin
        and Alan B. Durning.
_____ 83. **Reforesting the Earth** by Sandra Postel and Lori Heise.
_____ 84. **Rethinking the Role of the Automobile** by Michael Renner.
_____ 85. **The Changing World Food Prospect: The Nineties and Beyond** by Lester R. Brown.
_____ 86. **Environmental Refugees: A Yardstick of Habitability** by Jodi L. Jacobson.
_____ 87. **Protecting Life on Earth: Steps to Save the Ozone Layer** by Cynthia Pollock Shea.
_____ 88. **Action at the Grassroots: Fighting Poverty and Environmental Decline**
        by Alan B. Durning.
_____ 89. **National Security: The Economic and Environmental Dimensions** by Michael Renner.
_____ 90. **The Bicycle: Vehicle for a Small Planet** by Marcia D. Lowe.
_____ 91. **Slowing Global Warming: A Worldwide Strategy** by Christopher Flavin
_____ 92. **Poverty and the Environment: Reversing the Downward Spiral** by Alan B. Durning.
_____ 93. **Water for Agriculture: Facing the Limits** by Sandra Postel.
_____ 94. **Clearing the Air: A Global Agenda** by Hilary F. French.
_____ 95. **Apartheid's Environmental Toll** by Alan B. Durning.
_____ 96. **Swords Into Plowshares: Converting to a Peace Economy** by Michael Renner.
_____ 97. **The Global Politics of Abortion** by Jodi L. Jacobson.
_____ 98. **Alternatives to the Automobile: Transport for Livable Cities** by Marcia D. Lowe.
_____ 99. **Green Revolutions: Environmental Reconstruction in Eastern Europe and the Soviet Union**
        by Hilary F. French.

_____100. **Beyond the Petroleum Age: Designing a Solar Economy** by Christopher Flavin
        and Nicholas Lenssen.
_____101. **Discarding the Throwaway Society** by John E. Young.
_____102. **Women's Reproductive Health: The Silent Emergency** by Jodi L. Jacobson.
_____103. **Taking Stock: Animal Farming and the Environment** by Alan B. Durning and
        Holly B. Brough.
_____104. **Jobs in a Sustainable Economy** by Michael Renner.
_____105. **Shaping Cities: The Environmental and Human Dimensions** by Marcia D. Lowe.
_____106. **Nuclear Waste: The Problem That Won't Go Away** by Nicholas Lenssen.
_____107. **After the Earth Summit: The Future of Environmental Governance**
        by Hilary F. French.
_____108. **Life Support: Conserving Biological Diversity** by John C. Ryan.
_____109. **Mining the Earth** by John E. Young.
_____110. **Gender Bias: Roadblock to Sustainable Development** by Jodi L. Jacobson.
_____111. **Empowering Development: The New Energy Equation** by Nicholas Lenssen.
_____112. **Guardians of the Land: Indigenous Peoples and the Health of the Earth**
        by Alan Thein Durning.
_____113. **Costly Tradeoffs: Reconciling Trade and the Environment** by Hilary F. French.
_____114. **Critical Juncture: The Future of Peacekeeping** by Michael Renner.
_____115. **Global Network: Computers in a Sustainable Society** by John E. Young.
_____116. **Abandoned Seas: Reversing the Decline of the Oceans** by Peter Weber.
_____117. **Saving the Forests: What Will It Take?** by Alan Thein Durning.
_____118. **Back on Track: The Global Rail Revival** by Marcia D. Lowe.

_____ **Total Copies**

☐ **Single Copy: $5.00**
☐ **Bulk Copies (any combination of titles)**
  ☐ 2–5: $4.00 ea.   ☐ 6–20: $3.00 ea.   ☐ 21 or more: $2.00 ea.

☐ **Membership in the Worldwatch Library: $30.00 (international airmail $45.00)**
  The paperback edition of our 250-page "annual physical of the planet,"
  State of the World 1994, plus all Worldwatch Papers released during
  the calendar year.

☐ **Subscription to *World Watch* Magazine: $20.00 (international airmail $35.00)**
  Stay abreast of global environmental trends and issues with our award-
  winning, eminently readable bimonthly magazine.

Please include $3 postage and handling per order.

Make check payable to Worldwatch Institute
1776 Massachusetts Avenue, N.W., Washington, D.C. 20036-1904 USA

                    Enclosed is my check for U.S. $_____

_____

name   **daytime phone #**

_____

address

_____

city   **state**   **zip/country**

                                                              WWP